To Pat v Ron
Christmas 2007.

Peak District
Landscapes

PHOTOGRAPHS BY
Simon Kirwan
TEXT BY
Jerome Monahan

MYRIAD
LONDON

First published in 2005 by
Myriad Books Limited
35 Bishopsthorpe Road
London SE26 4PA

Photographs copyright
© Simon Kirwan
Text copyright
© Jerome Monahan

ISBN 1 904 736 0 4 1

www.myriadbooks.com

Title page: Higger Tor from
Over Owler Tor.
Right: Kinder Scout looking
towards Kinder Reservoir

CONTENTS

CHAPTER ONE

The North Peaks 6

CHAPTER TWO

The Central Peaks 44

CHAPTER THREE

The East Peaks 70

CHAPTER FOUR

The South Peaks 94

CHAPTER FIVE

The West Peaks 106

Peak District Landscapes

I FIRST DISCOVERED the Peak District when I changed jobs, and moved to Chesterfield. At first, my journeys of discovery were guided by *The Good Pub Guide*, as Derbyshire is a treasure-trove for the real-ale drinker, and the supply of country pubs hidden away in the villages of the Peak District is seemingly inexhaustible.

As we drove around, I slowly began to acquire an understanding of the Peak District itself, and the diverse nature of the surrounding landscape – the peaty uplands of the Kinder Scout plateau; the gritstone edges of Stanage, Baslow, Froggat and Curbar; the vast reservoirs of Derwent and Ladybower; the Great Ridge leading from Mam Tor; Blue John, Speedwell and Peak Caverns – the cave systems around Castleton; the rocky outcrops of Hen Cloud and the Roaches, and the timeless serenity of Dovedale.

But the Peak District is not a wild landscape untouched by humanity. Everywhere you look is the evidence of the human hand, including quarries, mines and towns of the Industrial Revolution, all criss-crossed by canals and railways. I became acquainted with places like Cromford, home of Arkwright's Mill, Middleton Top, with its engine house and beam engine to haul wagons up the Middleton Incline on the Cromford & High Peak Railway, the viaduct at Monsal Head, and the 19th-century spa towns of Buxton and Matlock Bath, which today is still a honeypot for visitors and features a cable-car to whisk you to the top of the Heights of Abraham. The plague village of Eyam has its own poignant story.

The Peak District is also a walkers' paradise, and gradually I explored the countryside surrounding the villages. With my camping partner who shared my tent in Nepal, I walked along Doctor's Gate, along part of the Pennine Way, and up on to Kinder Scout, where you can occasionally stumble across wreckage from one of the 60-plus aircraft that have come to grief in that moorland wilderness.

From Hathersage, where the churchyard contains a gravestone claiming to mark the last resting place of Robin Hood's trusted deputy, Little John, I walked up to Over Owler Tor, from where you can see the ancient hill fort of Carl Wark and the raised plateau of Higger Tor. I walked the Great Ridge from Mam Tor to Lose Hill and camped at Edale, where Pennine Way walkers begin their long trek northwards.

Time moved on, I left Chesterfield, and found new places to visit, both in the United Kingdom, and further afield, but the Peak District retains its pull, and I am still finding new villages to visit, new rocky edges to scramble and new hills to roam.

During the photography for this book, I even managed to re-visit some classic country pubs, although my pilgrimage to The Olde Bulls Head in Little Hucklow ended in disappointment as it was closed on the day I visited – giving me one more reason to make yet another return journey to the Peak District.

Simon Kirwan

THE NORTH PEAKS

MOST OF THE North Peak is taken up with a vast area of moorland crossed by a single main road, the A57. It follows the course of a Roman road, running up the central Ladybower and Woodlands valleys and joining Glossop in the west and Sheffield in the east. This is an untamed landscape dominated by peat bogs and occasional gritstone outcrops on the "edges". Only the hardiest of walkers venture out onto the moors proper where the bogs are formidable and the going is distinctly heavy, though the reward of true solitude so near to major conurbations cannot be underestimated. This is the true "dark peak" dominated by brooding peat moorlands such as Kinder Scout (left) – site of one of the most famous acts of civil disobedience in modern times – and Bleaklow. Of course, the North Peak does not lack evidence of human influence and settlement. At Peveril Castle (above) today's ruins can only hint at the imposing presence this castle must have exerted over the locality – a reminder of the new status quo following the Norman victory at Hastings.

BRADFIELD

The picturesque village of Bradfield nestles in the Loxley Valley on the edge of the Peak District national park, about five miles from the centre of Sheffield. This lowland area is the source of Bradfield potatoes – one of many local varieties. The settlement is split between High and Low Bradfield and a number of outlying farms. As part of the national park, it is subject to stringent planning and building controls. These ensure the use of vernacular materials and the retention of original features in local buildings, enlivened, as seen below, by examples of topiary. High Bradfield has a 12th-century church and would once have been dominated by a local Norman stronghold to the west, that is still in evidence at Bailey Hill.

CHINLEY CHURN *(above)*

To the south-west of Bradfield is the village of Chinley, a few miles from Whaley Bridge and Buxton. It lies on a number of public rights of way and is the setting-off point for walkers and ramblers eager to explore the surrounding beauty spots including Cracken Edge and Eccles Pike. It is also the place to begin an exploration of Chinley Churn to the north. In this photograph the village of Chinley lies behind, while the view is towards Chinley Churn (1479ft/451m) across the fields.

LADYBOWER RESERVOIR

The Ladybower is one of three reservoirs constructed in the Upper Derwent Valley to supply water to Sheffield, Derby, Nottingham and Leicester. It was built between 1935 and 1943 and contains more than 6,000m gallons of water. There were casualties – namely the villages of Derwent and Ashopton, both submerged, their populations relocated. Much of the stone of Derwent's houses went to reinforce the dam, and Ashopton's site provides the foundations for the viaduct that carries the A57 over the reservoir (below right).

At times of drought the church in Derwent Village can be seen. The view (below left) is looking south-east down the east spur of the Ladybower from the Snake Pass. The heavily planted Woodlands valley shore east of the reservoir is in clear view.

THE DAMBUSTERS

Looking south down the upper spur of the Ladybower (left).
This photograph was taken from the parking spot just north
of the war memorial marking the practice runs of the
Dambusters before their daring wartime raid on the
Möhne, Sorpe and Eder dams in the Ruhr. Today it is
possible to take a helicopter ride along the training route
that the Dambusters squadron followed during their
practice runs in 1943.

LADYBOWER'S UPPER REACHES

The placid waters of the Ladybower in its upper reaches (left) taken from the Snake Pass before it starts its steep ascent over the High Peak. The Ladybower, Derwent and Howden Reservoirs are one of the Peak District's most popular tourist attractions, drawing in large numbers wanting to walk the gentle waterside paths, enjoy the view or take part in the water activities that have developed in recent years including angling, sailing and even scuba diving. While the bird-spotting potential is limited here the wilder land adjacent is home to meadow pipits, wrens, kestrels and even goshawks – a species undergoing a modest population revival in the Peaks.

DERWENT PUMPHOUSE

The Derwent Reservoir is formed by one of the three dams that help store the water of the Upper Derwent. Here can be seen the crenellated tower built to house vital pumping equipment. On cold or misty days these stretches of water become potentially mysterious places, made more so by the rumours of sightings of ghostly Second World War aeroplanes flying over the water and of a UFO crash-landing on Howden Moor in 1997.

PEVERIL CASTLE LOOKING TOWARDS MAM TOR AND LOSE HILL

Peveril Castle was built in 1080 by William Peveril, possibly the illegitimate son of William the Conquerer and one of his most trusted allies. It defended the royal hunting grounds in the area and also the local lead-mining industry. Henry II was responsible for building the keep in the 1170s. Originally access was probably gained from an external wooden staircase, now replaced by a modern spiral one. The exterior of the keep was faced with ashlar cladding, most of which has since been stripped but fragments have survived on the south-eastern wall, and some towards the tops of the other walls.

The castle saw a succession of visits by kings and queens but in the late 14th century it was granted to John of Gaunt, in exchange for the earldom of Richmond, and Peveril then became part of the Duchy of Lancaster. In Tudor times it was thought to be too uncomfortable for royal residence and it went into decline. The keep, however, was maintained as a courthouse. Peveril is at the heart of the Peak District, overlooking Castleton. It offers the visitor breathtaking views over the surrounding countryside, towards Mam Tor (above) and north over the fields around Castleton towards Lose Hill (right).

CAVEDALE

The sheer sides of Cavedale helped make the Norman Peveril Castle impregnable. Right: here the view is a westerly one, looking up the valley with the village of Castleton to the rear and, for those climbing the main ridge, views of Mam Tor beyond. On the north side of the Castle is Peak Cavern Gorge. Peak Cavern's entrance was known as the Devil's Arse and was considered to be one of the region's greatest wonders. Cavedale is a collapsed cavern and the very bottom part was covered by a natural arch until 200 years ago.

THE LIMESTONE WAY

In the sunshine this is a startling place, but it is not hard to imagine how intimidating it must once have seemed when Peveril Castle was garrisoned, protecting the king's nearby hunting grounds. Cavedale is now connected to the high ground of Old Moor to the south by the Limestone Way, a route that takes the visitor past numerous disused and hazardous mines.

CASTLETON VIEWS

The pretty little town of Castleton nestles at the foot of Mam Tor and guards the entrance to Winnats Pass and the dramatic Speedwell Cavern. It is a medieval village and is centred on its church, St Edmund's, and main square. The settlement was laid out on a grid pattern towards the end of the 12th century. St Edmund's was a victim of Victorian restoration, but its Norman arch across the nave survives. Built between 1190-1250, it is considered one of the finest churches in the region. Other signs of the Norman era still remain – across the road by the Bull's Head Inn you can see a section

of the Town Ditch, a defensive earthwork built around the village. Around Castleton's square are some fine old houses and cottages, including a youth hostel, a Peak National Park information centre, the George Inn and several houses which offer teas and/or bed-and-breakfast. On the main road there are rows of shops, but most of them sell only Blue John (a local variety of fluorspar with a fine colouring), jewellery made from this or souvenirs. One shop here houses the Ollerenshaw Collection, which contains a range of fine specimens of Blue John.

CASTLETON CAFE

The area around Castleton has been described as "the most educational of all landscapes". The village is situated at the top of the Hope Valley, on the border of the Dark and White Peak areas of the national park. The northern slopes of the valley are composed of shale and gritstone rocks, typical of the Dark Peak. The southern slopes rise to form a limestone plateau associated with the White Peak. The presence of Peverel Castle, the gorges and the limestone caves and caverns have also added to the area's attractions making it a major tourist hub, especially in the summer. And where there are tourists there is a need for tea and cakes and picturesque buildings in which to consume them. One of the most well-known of these in Castleton is the Three Roofs Café, located opposite the village's main car park.

The beautiful Odin Sitch (left) runs through the village, bordered by a drystone wall. The ancient Odin mine was located at the foot of Mam Tor from where silver and lead was extracted.

LITTLE JOHN

Tradition has it that Little John, perhaps the most famous of Robin Hood's merry men, was born in Hathersage, near Castleton. Legend has it that he fought at the Battle of Evesham in 1265 for Simon de Montefort. De Montefort was killed, and Little John and Robin Hood became outlaws. Years later Little John returned to the village to die. His gravestone in St Michael's Church marks the spot, it is said, that Little John chose for his burial by firing an arrow from "Robin Hood's Stoop", a landmark some miles away on the moors above Hathersage.

LOSE HILL

There is a highly enjoyable, though strenuous, 6.5 mile (10km) walk that takes in all the sights featured on this page. It starts in Castleton, takes the rambler across the Hope Valley to the gradually swelling shape of Lose Hill, rising to 1560ft (476m) above sea level. At the summit a stone way-marker (right) surmounted by an engraved brass plate can be seen. It carries information about all the surrounding scenery. Admiration of the High Peak moors to the north over, it is time to take the route south-west travelling along Barker Bank to by-pass Mam Tor (above).

WINNATS PASS

A zig-zagging path brings the walker onto the spectacular limestone gorge of Winnats Pass. Despite the presence of the Sheffield to Chapel-en-le-Frith road it is not hard to believe the local legend of murder and fate associated with this spot. Legend has it that the killers of a young eloping couple in 1758 here all met untimely ends. The walk goes full circle, taking in Peverel Castle on the way and returning the tired explorer to Castleton for tea.

Winnats Pass is the only route out of the head of Hope Valley for vehicles. The road climbs to 1300ft (396m) through a narrow gorge, hemmed in by high limestone cliffs on either side. At the lower end of the pass is Speedwell Cavern, where you can visit ancient undergound mineworkings by boat.

MAM TOR

Mam Tor dominates the Hope Valley. With its softly undulating shape, it was given its name by the Celts – the "Mother Mountain". The remains of a 16-acre Iron Age hill fort underline how important the mountain was to the ancient people of the region. The track that connects the 1700ft (518m) summit to that of Lose Hill to the north is now maintained and paved with limestone, a route along which a seemingly endless succession of walkers, young and old, make their way.

THE SHIVERING MOUNTAIN

Mam Tor's other nickname is "the Shivering Mountain", testament to the instability of the sedimentary rocks from which it is formed. The sandstone and shale combination is highly friable causing the slopes to crumble. One of the most spectacular recent rockfalls occurred in 1979, effectively sealing the fate of the old route of the A625, trans-Pennine road, forcing it to take its current course over Winnats Pass.

AN IRON AGE HILL FORT

History does not record when the rock fall that created the spectacular eastern exposed face of Mam Tor occurred, but it was likely to have been a moment when the peak earned its reputation as the "shivering mountain". The area below the face is unstable and when rainfall has been heavy the shale is undermined and crumbles, causing sections of the strata to slip down into the valley. The trig point marked by a cemented stone cairn (below) on the summit of the hill is placed on top of a tumulus which probably dates from the Bronze Age; a bronze axehead was one of the finds from the site. The Iron Age fort is still easily made out. The ramparts are obvious and there are clear remains of two gateways on the paths leading from Mam Nick and from Hollins Cross. Hut circles have been found within the defences. These plus numerous pottery finds suggest this was a village rather than an occasionally garrisoned fortification.

As well as the spectacular views, Mam Tor is a local centre for hang-gliding, with enthusiasts taking advantage of the winds that continuously buffet this exposed spot.

THE PENNINE WAY

It is arguably the most famous of all England and Wales' national trails. The Pennine Way is a 268 mile (430km) path that starts in the Peak District National Park, joins the Pennine ridge, passes through the Yorkshire Dales, continues up into Northumberland, traverses the Cheviots and eventually ends in the Scottish Borders. It is described as a "grand traverse of the backbone of England" and takes a fit walker about 16 days to complete.

THE LAST CHANCE SALOON

The Nag's Head is the last refreshment stop for walkers
stepping out on the Pennine Way from Edale – a place
where heavy boots and Labradors are welcome, both still
free of the heavy peat that will soon be weighing heavy on
feet and paws alike.

   The little village of Edale was really put on the map after
the construction of a railway link between Manchester and
Sheffield. Previously the valley had been reserved for royal
hunting and sheep farming. In the 20th century its name
became inextricably linked to the right of access campaign
culminating in the mass trespass on Kinder Scout in 1932.

DOCTOR'S GATE *(below)*

It is hard to imagine that this area, now dotted with walkers in all but the mos
savage weather, spent over a century out of bounds to anyone but the land's o
thanks to an Act of Enclosure in 1836. That we can now wander this stunning spot –
a 15 mile (24km) plateau of wind and ice-shattered boulders, peat bogs and gr
some resembling First World War trenches – is thanks in large part to 400 walk
and their mass trespass of April 24 1932. The event was specifically mentioned in t
1945 Dower Report that lead to the creation of the UK's national parks. An o
Roman road brings one to Doctor's Gate – the name derived from a 16th-cent
Glossop medical man who travelled this route.

KINDER DOWNFALL *(right)*

Kinder Scout is thought to derive its name from the Saxon for "water over the edg
or *kyndwr scut*. Nowhere is this more appropriate than at Kinder Downfall, w
most of the plateau's water gathers to drop over 8oft (24m). In windy conditions,
the famous "blow back" effect occurs, with the water being pushed skyward. In t
winter the flow can freeze, creating a ribbon of refracting silver against the dar
slopes of the Kinder Downfall amphitheatre.

KINDER: THE WESTERN EDGE

"The dark and brooding Kinder massif stands at the foot of the Pennine Chain, a long tongue of relatively wild and untamed terrain probing south towards England's lowlands", writes naturalist Stephen Trotter. Kinder is made up of a number of distinct habitats including upland heath boasting heather, bilberry and crowberry and blanket peat bog on the plateau. Prominent everywhere are the tors that break through the surface seemingly shaped by artists' hands more than the action of wind, ice and rain on rock.

Overleaf:
Shelf Moor in winter. Kinder Scout and Shelf Moor face each other across the Snake Pass – the A57 Glossop to Sheffield road

KINDER NEAR SANDY HEYS

Writing in 1908, JB Firth said of Kinder:
". . . great boulders stand up on the summit, jagging the skyline, and at intervals along the steep precipitous sides there are clefts from top to bottom, some so deep as to resemble chasms with bare sides and courses for torrents in their stony beds. The whole vast ridge, whose wonderful beauty of outline and form and mass contrasts delightfully with the moody moors . . ."

36

THE MASS TRESPASS

JB Firth knew Kinder at a time when the place was off limits to all but the
invited guests of local landowners. All was to begin to change with the
mass trespass of 1932 when 400 men, women and children, organised by
the British Workers' Sports Federation, set out onto Kinder from Hayfield.
This was just one among many organised trespasses in the 1930s but it
became the most celebrated. In 1982 a plaque was unveiled in Bowden
Bridge Quarry, near Hayfield, where the 400 originally gathered.

   The Peak District lies below busy skies and has been the site of many
plane disasters, particularly during the war when bombers returning from
night raids would become lost over the dark landscape. Here, right,
wreckage of a plane emerges from the peat bog of Kinder Scout.

UPPER HOUSE

Drystone walls and rich pasture characterise the farmland lying around the wooded area to the west of the upper reaches of the River Kinder.

KINDER RESERVOIR

The River Kinder's flow now contributes to the expanse of water that is Kinder Reservoir, a beautiful backdrop no doubt for the fortunate residents of Upper House (far left). Construction of the Kinder Reservoir and its much-photographed circular filter house (left) was completed in 1911. Built from local stone and clay, the reservoir was created to supply nearby Stockport. In order to transport the building materials to this remote spot, a special railway spur was created, but the two-mile track and the "tin town" of workers' shacks that sprang up just north of Bowden Bridge have both vanished now.

ROUTE TO THE TOP

The William Clough is the name of the path up the side of Kinder Reservoir to the high ground above. This was the route taken by the 1932 Kinder Scout trespassers. It was from here that the walkers mounted their assault on the slopes of Sandy Heys, intending to reach the plateau above. They were met by about 20 gamekeepers and some brief struggles broke out. A victory celebration was held near Ashop Head and the group then made their way back into Hayfield where the police arrested six people, two of whom ended up charged with riotous assembly.

WATERFALL, WILLIAM CLOUGH *(right)*

The descent of William Clough takes walkers past a number of delightful small waterfalls and pools which occur along the way.

BROWN KNOLL

Brown Knoll is a high spot 1866ft (569m) above sea level which marks the join of a spur of millstone branching off from the Kinder massif and which forms the southern edge of the Edale Valley. The photograph above was taken above the Hayfield Road looking north-east. There are spectacular views down the Edale Valley from Brown Knoll.

HAYFIELD

In the Domesday Book it was referred to as "Hedfeld". Its main river is the Sett, which played a key role in Hayfield's industrial past. It is hard to believe, wandering this picturesque place, that it was once a home to wool and cotton manufacture, paper-making and textile printing. The Sett has also been a curse, flooding the village on a number of occasions, even disinterring corpses from the graveyard.

In 1932, Hayfield cricket ground was the meeting place of the 400 ramblers intent on performing the mass trespass on Kinder Scout – a key moment in the "right to roam" campaign.

THE CENTRAL PEAKS

THE CENTRAL PART of the Peak District National Park is often described as the "White Peak", due to the prominence of limestone deposited in the Carboniferous period about 350 million years ago. It was laid down before the development of the gritstone moors and gives an altogether gentler landscape. Its fields and woods are linked by over 26,000 miles of drystone walls. It is an area of important settlement and history – not least at Eyam, where the population made perhaps one of the most selfless acts in recent history to safeguard their neighbouring villages from death and disease.

BUXTON – THE PAVILION GARDENS

The elegant spa town of Buxton occupies a hollow at the southern end of the Pennines. Here limestone and gritstone meet and the underlying strata allows for the creation of thermal springs that have long been the source of the town's fortunes. Buxton has been a place of pilgrimage for those seeking cures for their ills ever since Roman times. The Romans established a settlement here called *Aquae Arnemetiae*. The Pavilion Gardens (above) were established in 1871 by Edward Milner, a pupil of Sir Joseph Paxton of Chatsworth and Crystal Palace fame. As well as the beautiful greenhouses, these 23 acres of Victorian landscaping on the banks of the River Wye include the Octagon – today often used for antique fairs.

BUXTON – THE CRESCENT

The town's more recent success was engineered by the 5th Duke of Devonshire, responsible for the building of the fashionable Crescent (above) around the main spring and the Great Stables (1789), later to become part of the Devonshire Royal Hospital and now part of the University of Derby.

PAVILION GARDENS HOTHOUSE

Buxton entered a period of decline in the 1970s and 80s but its fortunes are on the ascendancy again, thanks in part to the town's annual music festival, centred on the Edwardian Opera House, which is located in 25 acres of ornamental gardens at the heart of the town. The gardens also accommodate ornamental waters, a pavilion and concert hall, a theatre and reading rooms.

The hothouse (right) is home to numerous tropical and sub-tropical plants, providing a refuge from the winter cold. The next door Octagon was originally a concert hall designed by Robert Rippon Duke. The building is a great gathering point for locals and visitors alike and has long been associated with antique and trade fairs. It is claimed that a journalist coined the phrase "Beatlemania" here in 1963 in response to the furore surrounding the band.

BUXTON TOWN CENTRE

Buxton has had a rich history. A hall was erected over the main bath by George Talbot, 6th Earl of Shrewsbury. It was used to accommodate visitors and also the occasional prisoner including Mary Queen of Scots. She is said to have "taken the waters" to help her with her rheumatism. Daniel Defoe was here in the late 17th century but remained unimpressed by the nearby Poole's Cavern, describing it as "another of the wonderless wonders of the Peak". Today, the high street has been pedestrianised and spruced up, and is an attractive place for visitors to wander and to appreciate the beautiful streetscape.

MONSAL HEAD VIADUCT

The railway viaduct was built in 1863 and attracted its share of opprobrium. Writing in the 1870s, the critic and social reformer John Ruskin quipped that, thanks to the structure, "the valley is gone and the Gods with it and now every fool in Buxton can be in Bakewell in half an hour and every fool in Bakewell in Buxton". The viaduct is a superb example of Victorian engineering. It has been disused since 1968 and is now part of the Monsal Trail.

THE MONSAL TRAIL

The River Wye rises in the millstone plateau west of Buxton, passing through some spectacular limestone scenery before joining the River Derwent at Rowsley. Among the several Dales it crosses is Monsal Dale. There are a number of weirs along the river's length which add to the delights on offer to walkers following the nine-mile Monsal Trail. It runs from the Coombs Road viaduct, about a mile south of Bakewell to Blackwell Mill junction, three miles or so from Buxton.

MONSAL HEAD VIADUCT

The Monsal Trail follows the course of the old Midland Railway through the very heart of the Peak District. The building of the line was opposed by the Dukes of Devonshire and Rutland, coming too close for comfort to their estates. Devonshire refused it access entirely to the grounds of Chatsworth Park; his neighbour, Rutland, struck a deal whereby the railway was hidden from Haddon Hall thanks to the construction of a tunnel. Today, the viaduct has blended into the scenery and would be missed were it to vanish. The views it provides up the Monsal valley are some of the most spectacular in the national park.

ASHFORD-IN-THE-WATER

Ashford's presence in the Domesday Book underlines its ancient origins. Its beauty is enhanced by the River Wye, its main attraction being the "sheep wash" bridge. This was a medieval packhorse bridge where, until recently, sheep were washed prior to shearing. The lambs would be placed in the stone-walled pen on one side of the river, and the mothers would be thrown in at the other side. Their lambs' bleats would force them to swim across the river giving their coats a thorough soaking.

In the 19th century Ashford was famous for the black marble so beloved by the Victorians for fireplaces, vases and jewellery. Many of the stone cottages in the village served as workshops for its production before the marble works were established by a Bakewell man, Henry Watson, in 1748.

ASHFORD'S ANCIENT TRADITIONS

An unusual custom that took place in the village was that of hanging funeral garlands from the roof of Holy Trinity Church. Four garlands still hang there, the oldest dating from 1747. Well-dressing also occurs each year in Ashford – a ritual which is a tribute to the local abundance of water. Six wells are dressed, by layering petals, leaves and other natural objects into a bed of clay to form an impressive picture.

Holy Trinity Church has many fine features including some dating back to the 13th century, in particular the lower part of the unbuttressed west tower and the south door with its original Norman tympanum showing a tree of life in the centre with a hog and wolf facing it.

MILLER'S DALE

The glory days of Miller's Dale are associated with the local railway junction where passengers for Buxton made their connections between London and Manchester on the old Midland Railway. In 1964 the station and line closed leaving the spot to sink into obscurity, except that it is now an ideal starting point for walkers eager to explore the local limestone scenery. The hamlet is still dominated by the massive railway viaducts across the Wye valley (right).

EXPLORING MILLER'S DALE

One route takes travellers down the platform and onto the cinder path on top of the former trackbed. One of the first things to be encountered is a disused limekiln (below). Downstream from the village lies Litton Mill, a small hamlet grouped around a former cotton mill. The mill was built in the late 18th century and was infamous for its

harsh treatment of its apprentices, many of whom were orphans and who died from the cruel regime they were forced to endure.

Miller's Dale is an excellent centre from which to explore the gorges of the Wye and the high limestone plateau around it. Ravenstor, towards Litton Mill, is a fearsome overhanging limestone cliff popular with climbers, and there is more rock-climbing in Cheedale, upstream.

Overleaf: a disused quarry above Cunningdale, just outside Buxton.

TIDESWELL

Tideswell's principal attraction all year round is the 14th-century Church of St John the Baptist. Known locally as "The Cathedral of the Peak", it is a tribute to the strength of the local economy in the Middle Ages.

The church has a beautiful high nave and a number of outstanding wooden carvings by the Hunstone family, a famous woodcarving family. Local poet William Newton, "the minstrel of the Peaks" is buried here.

TIDESWELL TRADITIONS

Tideswell, another of the lovely market towns of the Peak District, is situated about nine miles east of Buxton, within the national park. It is one of the most ancient settlements in the central Peak District. It was the site of the "Great Courts" of the Royal Forest of the Peak in the time of Edward I. The name is thought to have been inspired by a local resident who went under the name of "Tidde".

The village was a centre for the lead-mining industry from medieval times to the 19th century. It also had a weekly market during the same period but the Market Place is now the only remnant of that tradition.

One of Tideswell's main annual summer attractions is the carnival and well-dressing ceremony. This is a focus for the whole community and draws visitors from far and wide.

EYAM

Eyam is a wonderfully preserved Peak village. It is the famous "plague village", which went into voluntary quarantine when the plague was imported from London in 1665. Above the village lies Eyam Moor which is a fine area for walking, with good views across the Derwent Valley and many Bronze Age remains and monuments.

When the plague struck Eyam in 1665, brought there in a box of cloth or clothes from London, the village's rector, the Rev William Mompesson and Thomas Stanley persuaded the entire community to place itself in quarantine and thus managed to stop its spread to the surrounding area. Two years later 259 villagers were dead; many of the houses bear plaques commemorating those who succumbed to the disease.

THE CHURCH OF ST LAWRENCE

Once the plague struck, the Rev William Mompesson closed St Lawrence and services were held in Cucklett Delph, a small valley nearby. In August every year a thanksgiving service is held at Cucklett to mark their sacrifice. The fenced stone (left) was one of the places where supplies were left by people from neighbouring villages during Eyam's period of quarantine.

Many of Eyam's houses have plaques giving details of their history and the part their inhabitants played in the plague saga. On the main street lies Eyam Hall (right) built in 1676 but in a style which was already out of fashion, so it looks like an early Jacobean mansion. It is the home of the Wright family who built it and have lived there ever since, and it is open to visitors in the summer months.

HIGGER TOR

The landscape is surreal, almost lunar on Higger Tor, where rounded rocks perch delicately one on top of another as if placed there by human hand. The landscape beyond is boggy and hard-going though home to many small birds, mammals and many varieties of water-loving wild plant.

Carl Wark is a remarkable escarpment hill fort. Over 984ft (300m) high, it makes use of natural sheer cliffs on three sides to provide an easily defended position. This is a hill fort the origins of which are still contested – it could date from either the Iron or Dark Ages. Bronze Age artefacts are also close by and show a long general occupation of the area.

Carl Wark appears to occupy a significant position and may well have figured in the defence of their land by the Brigantes, a local tribe at the time of the Roman invasion of Britain.

Overleaf:
A view of Carl Wark from Over Owler Tor

65

TWO VIEWS OF OVER OWLER TOR

Walkers describe this landscape as "rounded". Over Owler Tor lies about 1246ft (380m) above sea level and gives spectacular views of the surrounding landscape. Here, the sights to the north-west include the town of Hathersage and the River Derwent. Parts of the Hope Valley near Hathersage are thought to have been the inspiration for sections of *Jane Eyre*. Charlotte Bronte was a friend of Ellen Nussey, whose brother was the vicar of Hathersage and she was their visitor in 1845.

Directly east of Over Owler Tor is a flattened plateau of rocks and heather. It is a lonely spot now, but evidence of earlier settlement and use abounds including signs of an ancient field system and quarries. Rocks here are etched and eroded by wind and rain to appear almost made by hand. The Peaks stand at a natural crossroads marking the meeting place of highland and lowland creating a fascinating overlap of both flora and fauna.

THE EAST PEAKS

THIS IS IS AN AREA of richly contrasting scenery encompassing rolling farmland, remote moors and "edges" – those spectacular steep escarpments that typify the region and hint at the powerful forces that have governed its geology over the millennia. It is a landscape of river scenery too being crossed by the Derwent and the Wye. The Derwent passes through and near towns picturesque now, Cromford and Matlock, but once the cradle of this nation's burgeoning commercial strength, playing a pivotal role in the Industrial Revolution.

BAKEWELL BRIDGE
Little survives of medieval Bakewell today except the town's early 14th-century bridge with its row of five typically Gothic arches. The bridge is still in use and is thought to be one of the oldest in Britain. It is a reminder of the town's origins as a key route over the River Wye for the wool drovers and merchants.

BLACK ROCK
Climbers work their way up a joint in the gritstone cliff known as the Black Rock. The site dominates the horizon above the town of Cromford near the limestone crags of High Tor and Wild Cat. This is a landscape of evocative place names, born of Victorian whimsy more than ancient tradition. Black Rock, though not as popular with climbers as some of the other crags in the east and southern Peaks, still boasts some nerve-jangling ascents in the higher sections up its blank arêtes and walls.

BAKEWELL VIEWS FROM THE BRIDGE

The view west from medieval Bakewell bridge takes in the rippling waters of the
River Wye looking up-river towards the beautiful 17th-century Holme Hall. The
Wye connects Bakewell with Buxton, its route between the two towns carved
through a series of gorges. At Bakewell, the river has matured into an altogether
gentler waterway. Beyond Bakewell, the Wye passes the exquisite Tudor Haddon Hall
and its gardens – home to the Dukes of Rutland. From there it has only a short
distance to go before it joins the River Derwent at Rowsley.

A mid river island (right) adds to the picturesque south-easterly view from
Bakewell's medieval arched bridge. The riverside water gardens are a favourite spot
for local people and visitors and a sizeable population of geese. It is hard to imagine
the Wye in this gentle spot negotiating the far wilder scenery that defines its passage
to this point from its emergence at Poole's Cavern, near Buxton, through the gorges
of Ashwood Dale and Cheedale. The Wye has also a long history serving the needs of
industry, and old mills and factories line its banks.

RIVER WYE

The Wye is a popular fishing river, frequently stocked
to provide sport for syndicates, hotels and others
prepared to pay for fly-angling licenses. The limestone
that characterises much of the Eastern Peaks enriches
the river with nutrients and preserves its alkaline
nature. This leads to an abundance of insect life,
thriving in the rich weed beds. The Wye trout quickly
grow fat on a continual banquet of shrimps, sedges,
flies and many other invertebrates.

BAKEWELL TARTS

While Bakewell has one of the oldest markets in the area, dating from at least 1300, one item for sale today has more recent origins. The famous "Bakewell pudding" (often called "Bakewell tart" in error) was first created in 1860 when a cook employed by a Mrs Greaves at the Rutland Arms Hotel confused her pie-making instructions. Mrs Greaves left the recipe in her will. Today it figures prominently for sale on signs outside the town's many bakeries.

BAKEWELL, SCOTTS GARDENS

The Domesday book entry calls the town *Badequella*, meaning Bath-well. It has grown up at a "landform boundary" between limestone to the west and gritstone to the east. The town is blessed with beautiful riverside walks and meadows. One of the most picturesque and popular is known as Scotts Gardens. The meadow was given to the town in the early 1930s. On crisp, bright days the trees in this and other spots along the river walks are redolent of landscapes by the Impressionist painter Corot.

THE WEIR

It is possible for walkers to pause and admire the weir just downriver from Bakewell's medieval bridge as they explore the riverside route through the town. Here the "fall" created by the weir is gentle, its sound a calming antidote to the traffic of the town, swelled these days by a stream of visitors. In summer, with bankside trees masking the landscape beyond, it is easy to imagine oneself on an entirely rural section of the River Wye, instead of just a few hundred paces from the hurly-burly of Bakewell – the East Peak's unofficial "capital".

BLACK ROCK

An outcrop of gritstone sculpted by the wind and rain, Black Rock hangs high above the historic town of Cromford with Cromford Moor behind and the High Peak Trail (the former Cromford and High Peak Railway) passing just below. It is a spectacular situation which affords a splendid view of the Derwent valley to the north and the altogether more populated area around Wirksworth to the south-west. The area has been designated a country park and is a popular place for recreation, with rock-climbing and plenty of scope for walking in the park, which stretches right down to High Peak Junction where the former railway met the Cromford canal. There is also a fixed orienteering course and forest trails in the surrounding woods. The country park has a car park and small information centre with public toilets.

The gritstone from which Black Rock has been formed is a coarse, hard sandstone. It has been described as "God's own rock" – a tribute to its variety. It is a rock capable of producing everything from gentle boulders to fierce "flaring" outcrops much favoured by climbers.

MIDDLETON

Anyone walking the 17.5 mile (28km) High Peak Trail is actually following the route of the now abandoned Cromford and High Peak Railway. The industrial heritage of this area can never be far from the mind as the way is peppered with evidence of sidings, engine houses, signals, shafts and quarries. One of the most substantial of these occurs just to the west of the village of Middleton, now long abandoned and steadily being colonised by wild flowers and grasses. The quarry's steep sides are reminiscent of a mini-canyon, while the rock strewn but daisy-covered pavement calls to mind Alpine landscapes.

LEAD MINES AND QUARRIES

In the 17th and 18th centuries fortunes were made by those in the East Peaks with control of lead-mining. The industry went into decline in the 19th century, as the shafts went deeper and deeper, became prone to flooding and finally lost out to more easily-mined Australian lead. The landscape around Wirksworth and Middleton still bears the scars. Even more noticeable are the limestone quarries, sunk into the local hills and mountains in response to the needs of agriculture and industry. Both towns suffered significant dust and noise pollution, but with the closure of the quarries and concerted action to improve the environment, the area is enjoying a rebirth as a popular tourist destination. Middleton Top now boasts a visitors' centre celebrating the area's industrial heritage.

MIDDLETON TOP

The view south from Middleton Top catches the grandeur of a landscape where blue distant hills meet the sky and sunshine periodically illuminates the fields of the Wirksworth valley far below, where the pattern of drystone walls has remained unchanged for centuries. Middleton Moor is over 1148ft (350m) above sea level at its highest point and is surrounded by steep escarpments falling to the

Via Gellia to the north, and a network of encroaching quarries to the east, west and south. The nearby village of Middleton has a rich literary heritage to match its industrial history, having been home to DH Lawrence. He used the village as inspiration for Woodlinkin, the backdrop to events in his novella *The Virgin and the Gypsy* – discovered in 1930 in France among his possessions following his death.

MIDDLETON TOP ENGINE HOUSE

Situated at the top of the Middleton Incline on the High Peak Trail is the restored Middleton Top Engine House, which was built in 1829. It continues to house the machinery once used to haul wagons up the Middleton Incline. They were pulled a distance of 708 yards up a gradient of 1 in 8.5, for 134 years, finally being retired in 1963. The railway owes its existence to a failed scheme to build a canal system here linking the East Midlands with Manchester, by-passing the Trent and Mersey Canal. The canal was never built due to technical difficulties, one of the main reasons being the lack of water on the limestone plateau.

RICHARD ARKWRIGHT AND CROMFORD

The history of Cromford is intertwined with that of the entrepreneur and early industrial magnate Richard Arkwright (1732-1792). He financed the creation of a spinning frame, powered by a water wheel and set up a factory in 1771 in Cromford near the Derwent. The machinery became known as a "water frame". The town's fortunes were further underpinned by the development of canal transport. Cromford Canal opened in 1793, running 15 miles to Langley Mill where it linked with the Erewash Canal. It vastly improved access to the markets of Liverpool and Nottingham. Cotton fibres, textiles, limestone and lead were all transported on barges. Shown in the picture above is Cromford Mill's factory-side canal spur and covered loading quay.

WORKER'S COTTAGES, CROMFORD

Richard Arkwright did more than build factories in Cromford, he also imported the population needed to work in them, preferring weavers with large families – the women and children labouring in the spinning-factory, the weavers toiling at home turning the yarn into cloth. He provided them with homes, but expected his workers to maintain a punishing regime working from six in the morning to seven at night. Unlike some factory owners, Arkwright chose not to employ children under six in his factories, though after that age they were deemed sufficiently old to join the workforce. Two-thirds of Arkwright's 1,900 workers were children. Arkwright's fortune when he died was estimated at £500,000 – a fabulous sum. Via Gellia House (below left) and the adjacent row of three-storey houses was built by Nathaniel Wheatcroft around 1780. The Wheatcroft family operated the canal boats from Cromford Wharf.

RIBER CASTLE
(left) AND
MATLOCK BATH

The development of Matlock Bath as a major spa is due to the entrepreneurial flair of John Smedley (1803-1872). He developed the town's potential as a "hydro" to rival similar British and continental towns where ailing Victorians would come to "take the waters"; the photograph (right) of Matlock Spa, taken high above the Derwent, shows the Pump Room and the Matlock Pavilion, built in 1910.

Smedley constructed Riber Castle (left), for himself. Perched on a hill dominating the town, the house boasted electricity and gas at a time when such conveniences were still highly exotic. In the 20th century Riber Castle's fortunes were chequered – it was sold after the death of his widow in 1892 and was used as a public school until 1930. It became a food depot during the war and then, after being left empty for many years, it was the centrepiece of a nature reserve. In 2000 this also closed and the building entered another period of decline. Current plans include conversion into luxury flats.

MATLOCK: THE COUNTY TOWN

Matlock and Matlock Bath lie just outside the Peak District National Park, but Matlock is an important centre and Derbyshire's county town. The Romans may have mined lead here but the town was relatively unimportant until the early 19th century when it developed rapidly as a spa, hastened by the construction of the Midland Railway.

In the centre of the photograph (above) is the vast hydro, built by John Smedley in 1853. It functioned as a spa until the 1950s. Today, it is home to the county offices and the Derbyshire Dales Borough Council. Matlock is still a prominent tourist resort. Here we see the town photographed from the top of the Heights of Abraham.

THE DERWENT

Upriver from Matlock Bath, the Derwent is sufficiently rapid to attract canoeing enthusiasts, but by the time it reaches the town, it is far calmer allowing for the hire of pleasure boats. The picturesque scene is enhanced by the gracefully arching pedestrian bridge over the Derwent. The town's setting is distinctly Alpine, with the river's steep and wooded valleys creating a highly picturesque scene. The similarity was not lost on the Victorians who built the railway station at Matlock Bath in 1849 to resemble a Swiss chalet.

HEIGHTS OF ABRAHAM

The Alpine feel of Matlock Spa is further boosted by the presence of a hard-working cable car, carrying visitors up the 450ft (137m) incline to the Heights of Abraham. The name derives from the site of General Wolfe's victory and death at Quebec in 1759; it was chosen by local people because the narrow gorge of the River Derwent was said to resemble that of the St Laurence River.

Whereas Matlock (the town) is fairly open, Matlock Bath lies in a gorge. There are magnificent views of the gorge for those taking the cable car. Mining has played an important part in the development of the area and the Heights of Abraham has two impressive show caves: Grand Masson Cavern and the Great Rutland Cavern-Nestus Mine, where a little of the mining history of the area can be found. "Nestus" was the Roman name for Matlock. From the Heights of Abraham, there are views from the Prospect Tower (a stiff climb of 54 steps) from where it is possible to see a fine view of the valley.

CURBAR EDGE AND BASLOW EDGE *(right)*

The Peaks owe their unique landscape mainly to two rock strata – limestone and millstone grit. The millstone grit, a sedimentary rock created from sand deposits sometimes fused with shale, creating its characteristic dark colour, is impermeable and has resisted weathering to create imposing "edges" fringing the limestone central and southern parts of the park. This phenomenon is arguably at its most spectacular north of Bakewell where Froggatt's Edge, Curbar Edge and Baslow Edge join in breathtaking sequence. The photograph below is of the view south from Curbar Edge up the Derwent valley and, right, one of Baslow Edge's imposing cliff faces.

THE PLATEAU ABOVE CURBAR EDGE

Behind Curbar Edge, the landscape becomes an elevated plateau. It is a bleak spot
now, but has clearly enjoyed human settlement and reverence since at least the
Bronze Age, its surface dotted with cairns, enclosures, the signs of early field systems
and at least one stone circle adjacent to Froggatt's Edge. Below this point lie the
villages of Curbar and Calver. The latter's surviving cotton mill, built by Richard
Arkwright, enjoyed recent fame, being used as the setting for a television drama
series about Colditz Castle.

Curbar suffered from the Great Plague in the 17th century in much the same way
as Eyam, although about 30 years earlier. On the moors there are the gravestones of
the Cundy family who lived at Grislowfield farm. There are also a number of tombs
just below the Wesleyan Reform Chapel, which are dated 1632.

THE SOUTH PEAKS

WRITING IN THE 1880s, John Ruskin declared: "It is only in the clefts of it, and the dingles, that the traveller finds his joy", dismissing the millstone plateaux of the Dark Peaks in cavalier fashion. His joy and that of literally hundreds of thousands of visitors each year was reserved for the steep-sided valleys carved from the exposed limestone associated with the White Peaks of the south and central part of the national park. This is a startling and colourful landscape, replete with history and opportunities to stand and stare in wonder.

DOVEDALE *(left)*
The River Dove rises on the southern side of Axe Edge and flows almost southwards to the boundary of the Peak. It represents the border between Derbyshire and Staffordshire for the whole of its length. The river is utterly beautiful and has been recognised as a source of the sublime for many centuries – not least here where Tissington Spires emerge from the trees. The Dove is also a famous trout-fishing river, long-associated with Izaak Walton. His book *The Compleat Angler*, published in 1653, records his experiences with line and rod when visiting his friend Charles Cotton at Beresford Hall near Hartington.

MILLDALE *(above)*
The little cottage encapsulates much of the charm of Milldale today. The Walton links are stronger still in the tiny hamlet. In the *The Compleat Angler* Milldale's bridge over the Dove is called Viator's Bridge, Viator being the name of one of the two participants in the angling conversations that comprise the book. The other is Pescator. In reality these were Charles Cotton and Walton himself.

SHARPLOW DALE AND THE RIVER DOVE

To the East of Dovedale lies Sharplow Dale (left), perhaps not as eye-catching as Dovedale but full of interest. The plunging, gradient-hugging drystone wall is entirely characteristic of the White Peak areas of the national park.

The River Dove derives its name from the old English word *dubo* meaning "dark". It runs south for 45 miles until it enters the Trent. It often marks the border between the contrasting limestone and shale geology of Derbyshire and Staffordshire. Even in the Victorian era it was a popular touring area and it remains one of the most visited parts of the Park. Dr Johnson, an early tourist, suggested that having seen Dovedale there was no need to go to the Highlands of Scotland. Above is the north-east view of the Dove from Thorpe Cloud.

BUNSTER HILL, DOVEDALE & THORPE CLOUD

From west to east of this panoramic view (right) we can see Bunster Hill, the entrance to Dovedale and Thorpe Cloud on the right-hand edge of the gap. The River Dove rises on the eastern side of Axe Edge and flows almost southwards to the boundary of the Peak. Axe Edge is a high gritstone moor, and the river sweeps steeply down to arrive at the limestone rock near Hollinsclough. Along its length the rocks resemble giant pieces of uplifted coral, which is more or less what the limestone strata are. The Victorians got to work providing a series of colourful names for every outcrop and cave along the Dove's length. These include the two cliffs known as the Celestial Twins; Raven's Crag; Reynards Cave and Tissington Spires.

DOVEDALE *(below)*

The stepping stones at the entrance to Dovedale are best avoided in summer when its charms may be spoiled by hordes of tourists. But from this vantage point to the south, the landscape recovers some of its dignity.

ASHBOURNE

Known as the "Gateway to Dovedale", Ashbourne has had the right to hold a market since 1257 and was made a royal borough in 1276. The main place of interest in Ashbourne is Church Street, with its fine Georgian houses, old grammar school, almshouses and St Oswald's Church with its magnificent spire. One 17th-century house bears a plaque celebrating the visit of Dr Samuel Johnson. Here is shown the famous inn sign for the Green Man and Black's Head Hotel. It spans the street, underlining the amalgamation of the two coaching inns in 1825.

CARSINGTON WATER

One of Britain's younger generation of reservoirs, Carsington Water has become a great attraction since its opening in 1992 by HM The Queen. The reservoir is owned and operated by Severn Trent Water. It takes and stores water pumped from the River Derwent at times of high rainfall. The reservoir's visitors' centre contains a permanent exhibition explaining the essential role water plays in our lives. In the courtyard is the Kugel Stone, a ball of granite weighing over 1 tonne and which revolves on a thin film of water under pressure. The views here showing the reservoir, its resident population of swans and geese and the hills beyond are taken looking to the east.

CARSINGTON LEISURE

Carsington Water has quickly established itself as a premier leisure spot in the Peaks. Boating, fishing and birdwatching are all catered for. There is also a seven-mile waterside path, enhanced by the planting of half a million trees and shrubs which are now maturing. The facilities also include bird hides and a wildlife centre. There were sightings in the period immediately after the reservoir's opening of the Carsington Beast – a black big cat. It avoided capture!

STONES ISLAND

Stones Island is another landscaping feature created at Carsington since the opening of the reservoir. It reflects the Derbyshire tradition of creating hill-top monuments and was designed by Lewis Knight. Each of the stones relates to the surrounding countryside. There are toe-holds on every pillar allowing children to get some purchase and so enjoy the views too.

Carsington Village lies nearby. It contains a preaching cross, said to have been set up by a monk named Betti. The Carsington Church of St Margaret is of 12th-century origin but was rebuilt in 1648 in Gothic-style and stands on the bottom slopes of Carsington Pastures. For many years no building of any kind took place, but the arrival of Carsington reservoir has changed all that. New houses have been built in the village and barns belonging to the farms along the valley have been converted into homes.

MILLDALE

Milldale, situated in the Peak District National Park, is a peaceful riverside village of square stone cottages, surrounded by steeply wooded hills. The village is only visited by local traffic and walkers (above). The hamlet's name derives from an old corn mill situated here but demolished in the mid 19th century. The foundations can still be seen and so can the pool where local farmers washed their sheep in the river prior to shearing – this practice only ceased here in the 1960s.

Milldale provides a good starting point for walks in the Peak District around Dovedale to the south and Wolfscote Dale to the north. The famous packhorse bridge, over the river Dove, that links Milldale to Dovedale is called Viator Bridge, named after a character in the second part of *The Compleat Angler* by Izaak Walton.

THE WEST PEAKS

ALL OVER THE NORTH and west Peaks travellers encounter abandoned rounded rocks called millstones – they are the emblem of the Peak District National Park and give their name to the distinctive "millstone grit" rocks of the Pennines. The west peaks are fringed with particularly dramatic "edges" – the landscape at the Roaches and Ramshaw Rocks, where the "finger stone" (right) cleaves the sky are two of the best-known. The edges are made more dramatic because they overlook the Cheshire Plain and they are the first areas of high ground between the coast and the Peak District.

Millstone grit is a form of sandstone deposited by a great river system which spread out southwards from the Scottish Highlands around 320 million years ago, flooding over the older limestones. The river formed a delta by depositing layers of sand and mud. This cycle was repeated a number of times. As well as grindstones, the millstone grit sandstone has also been quarried for quality building stone. What little is still extracted is in great demand for restoration work on existing structures in the national park and beyond.

The West Peaks are interspersed with attractive tarns like the one above, on Goyt's Moss, adjacent to Goyt's Lane. It is possible to walk on the path on the far edge of the tarn, along the route of the former Cromford and High Peak Railway.

THE ROACHES

The Roaches, with Hen Cloud and
Ramshaw Rocks, form a gritstone
escarpment which marks the south-western
edge of the Peak. This is an area which is
under particular pressure from visitors. The
paths are popular with walkers, the cliffs
with climbers and the sky with hang-gliding
enthusiasts. The names of some of the cliff
routes known to climbers are colourful
including Saul's Crack, Valkyrie and the
Mangler. Up on top the landscape is
dominated by weirdly shaped rocks and
there are spectacular views of Tittesworth
Reservoir and the town of Leek, in
neighbouring Staffordshire.

DON WHILLANS AND THE ROACHES

At the southernmost foot of the Roaches is a small climber's hut, actually built into the cliff face and called Rockall Cottage. It has long been one of the area's main attractions, leading visitors to wonder at its precarious location beneath the imposing and overhanging gritstone rock face behind. The cottage is now a memorial to Don Whillans, the famous rock climber who pioneered many routes in the area.

THE ROACHES' WILDLIFE

They rise to over 474m above sea level and form one of the most impressive of the Western Peak's millstone grit "edges". The name is thought to derive from *les roches* – the French for "the rocks". The Roaches estate extends over 1,000 acres and was absorbed into the national park in 1979.

Visitors have in the past been surprised by encounters with members of a small colony of red-necked wallabies, descendants of escapees from a nearby game park. Although in Tasmania these wallabies range as high as 3000-4000 feet, the severe winter of 1962-3 in Britain almost wiped out the Peak colonies. There have not been sightings of the creatures for many years in the Roaches. One theory is that they have been preyed upon by another introduced alien species – one of the illegally released big cats that are said to prowl in various parts of the national park.

HEN CLOUD

Hen Cloud is a separate southern extremity of the Roaches. It rises spectacularly from the surrounding moor to 1555ft (410m) above sea level. This is the view north, looking back at the Roaches across the lowland gap that separates them. Hen Cloud overlooks the village of Upper Hulme. It is a reminder of how tough the conditions can become on these heights and the risks that even the most experienced climbers run.

HIGH EDGE

High Edge is a long gritstone edge that runs north to south on the moors above Sheffield University's research laboratories just south of Buxton. Nearer still are the Health & Safety Executive's Explosive Laboratory up on the moors themselves. As one walker suggests on his route notes for fellow ramblers: "Keep smiling as you are no doubt on camera."

RAMSHAW OUTCROPS

Ramshaw Rocks boast many wind and rain-etched outcrops, eroded into shapes suggestive of artistic endeavour. None more so than the "Finger Stone" which resembles a giant hand pointing an accusing digit heavenward. Its angle, typical of many of the exposed strata here, is due to the tilting of the bedding rock planes at this point. The moorland enclosed by the gritstone edges in this area produces run-off rivulets and streams that feed the waters of Tittesworth Reservoir to the south.

HIGHLAND CATTLE

Even the domestic beasts need to be well insulated to cope with the tough conditions locally either side of the summer months known to the majority of tourist visitors. Here shaggy Highland cattle keep a watchful eye on the proceedings, just south of the Ramshaw Rocks.

MACCLESFIELD

Macclesfield lies on the fringes of the Peak District. The earliest written reference to a settlement here is found in the Domesday Survey of 1086. Parts of the old town still retain their medieval street pattern.

MACCLESFIELD'S SILK INDUSTRY

Macclesfield became famous for its silk-making during the 17th century and today many of its attractions are connected with the textiles industry. The National Trust own two mills: Quarry Bank Mill & Styal Estate and Nether Alderley; and the Silk Museum, Paradise Mill and the Heritage Centre. The Silk Museum was once the base for the Macclesfield School of Art. Built in 1877 to train designers for the silk industry, it now houses exhibitions exploring the properties of silk, Macclesfield's diverse textile industries, workers' lives and historic machinery.

MACCLESFIELD AND THE SURROUNDING AREA

Macclesfield is a major shopping centre today, capable of pleasing even the most die-hard conspicuous consumer from the rich communities in and around Alderley Edge to the north. To the west of the town is the famous Jodrell Bank Observatory, which is run by Manchester University and is recognised as a leading radio-astronomy facility. To the south of Macclesfield is Gawsworth Hall, a Tudor manor house that once belonged to Mary Fitton, maid of honour to Elizabeth I. Mary fell swiftly from Her Majesty's favour after an affair with the Earl of Pembroke, which left her pregnant. She is one of the candidates for Shakespeare's "dark lady" of the Sonnets.

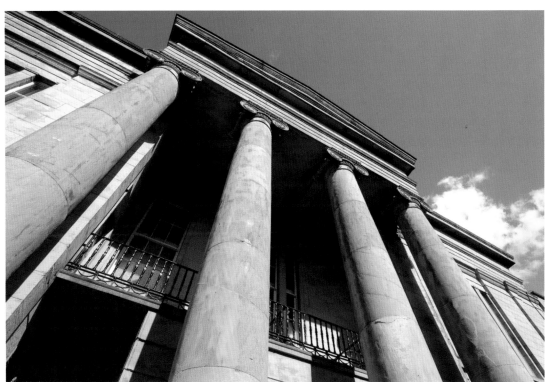

JENKIN CHAPEL

Jenkin Chapel's true name is the Church of St John the Baptist, Saltersford. The name is thought to derive from a drover who used to preach beside a nearby cross. Another story holds that the name refers to the "jinkin" sound of coins placed in the collection bag during services. The squat tower has a pitched roof and both were added on in 1754.

CAT & FIDDLE

The Cat and Fiddle Inn dates from 1830 and stands at over 1690ft (515m) above sea level. It is a favourite with walkers and coach-trippers, who only have to step outside with their pint to survey the spectacular view across the Cheshire Plain. Nearby, the river Goyt rises in the western Peak moorland.

FORMER CARPET MILL

Wildboarclough lays claim to being the site of the death of the last wild boar in England. The village is now a quiet backwater. There was once a carpet mill in the village that used the waters of Clough Brook to power its machinery. The mill was largely demolished but the administration block (above) remains – a fine building, which for a while enjoyed the status of being the largest sub-post office in England. The village is also home to Crag Hall – the country seat of Lord Derby.

EDINBORO COTTAGES

This attractive row of cottages stands on the valley road near Wildboarclough. They are just a few feet above Clough Brook and were flooded in 1989.

TEGG'S NOSE COUNTRY PARK

Master of all he surveys! A walker gets himself orientated thanks to a helpful map on the dolmen on top of Tegg's Nose (1148ft/350m) just east of Macclesfield. Before him stretches the view due west of the Cheshire plain and the Macclesfield Forest can also be seen from this point.

The area is a country park from which walkers can appreciate spectacular views including the Jodrell Bank telescope and Bollington. There is a nature trail here that takes visitors past meadows filled in season with mountain pansies and woodland filled with birdsong all year round.

A major drystone wall rebuilding project began here in 2002 using local stone and teams of volunteers including school and community groups.

Clouds on the horizon

Fluffy storm clouds build above the gentle summit to the east of Tegg's Nose. They are a reminder of how rapidly the weather can alter in the Peaks on even the most summery day. Macclesfield may be just four miles away, but apart from the occasional aeroplane or a hang-gliding enthusiast following an updraught, there is little otherwise to suggest one is not in the depths of the countryside.

Sheep gate

The country park is dotted with a number of imaginative environmental sculptures based on features which can be found in the surrounding Peaks. Here, a drystone wall has been formed into a gateway resembling a sheepfold. The gate is attractive and helps prevent animals straying across the fields.

GOYT VALLEY

The River Goyt drains off Axe Edge Moor and flows north, feeding both the Fernilee and Errwood Reservoirs on the way. The reservoirs opened in 1938 and 1967 respectively and led to the relocation of the 300-year-old packhorse bridge further down the valley. If you look up when visiting the area you may be rewarded with a sighting of one of the hen harriers recently returned to the Goyt Valley. These magnificent birds shared in the general collapse experienced by many raptor species in the 1950s, thanks in large part to over zealous gamekeeping.

GOYT VALLEY NEAR FERNILEE (left)

This photograph was taken just north of the Fernilee Reservoir looking across the Goyt Valley to the north. The beautiful triangular peak deserves a name but earns only gradient lines and a trig point on maps proclaiming its peak to be 843ft (257m) above sea level. The landscape beyond has many miles of open countryside before the next major settlements are reached – the villages of Whaley and Bollington, just outside the national park.

GOYT SCENERY (below)

This network of drystone walls and moorland fringes the slopes of the eastern edge of the Goyt Valley, a few miles south of Shallcross Hall Farm and is typical of Dark Peak scenery. The river Goyt rises on the moorland slopes near the Cat & Fiddle Inn between Buxton and Macclesfield and flows northwards through steep valleys to feed the Errwood and Fernilee Reservoirs. The valley's name derives from a local dialect word – *goyt* or *goit* – meaning a stream or watercourse.

GOYT'S LANE RESERVOIR

There are many small lakes in the Peaks which are characteristic of post-glacial scenery, filled with meltwaters and often circular in shape. Their icy water is often invitingly clear, particularly to the passing hill-walker on a hot summer's day. The view looks east with Goyt's Moss climbing to the left. The sky and its scudding clouds are reflected in the still surface of the tarn.

WINDGATHER ROCKS

Windgather Rocks owes its poetic name to the Victorians' mania for christening every outcrop and cave they discovered. On the day this photograph was taken the name was particularly appropriate as the open countryside was being lashed by stiff breezes bending the grasses in the fields to the west of the Goyt Forest.

ERRWOOD RESERVOIR

In the 1960s a second reservoir, Errwood (above and right) was built to supplement the supply already provided by the nearby Fernilee reservoir to Stockport. Errwood and its beautiful surroundings are popular with visitors and the reservoir frequently bristles with sails and its banks with picnic spots. The area is subject to strict vehicle controls as part of a visitor management system pioneered here and copied on reservoirs elsewhere in the Peaks.

The nearby Errwood Hall, to the west of the reservoir, was owned by the Catholic Grimshaw family, and was largely demolished at the time of the reservoir's construction. Its graveyard survives and includes a shrine built in memory of a well-loved Spanish governess to the family. The house was built in 1840 by Samuel Grimshaw who boasted that he had planted 40,000 rhododendrons around the estate. These are a wonderful sight in the spring and a great visitor attraction.

LAMALOAD RESERVOIR

Situated north of the A54 Buxton to Macclesfield road, close to the village of Rainow, within the Peak District National Park, the Lamaload Reservoir supplies drinking water to Macclesfield. To the east is the Goyt Valley. The reservoir was completed in 1964 and is approximately 1010ft (308m) above sea level. Fed by the river Dean, the water piles up behind an impressive, tall concrete dam. The landscape around Lamaload consists of moorland with a few plantations of larch and pine. Walkers heading for nearby Shining Tor enjoy spectacular views.

LANGLEY DISTRICT RESERVOIRS

Over 85 per cent of the north-west of England's fresh water derives from the Peak District's rivers, lakes and reservoirs. As well as the vast Derwent and Ladybower waters to the east there are more modest reserves in the western Peaks. The Leather's Smithy pub (far left), in the picturesque village of Langley, is close to three of these reservoirs. It faces the Ridgegate Reservoir and two others, the Bottoms Reservoir and the Tegg's Nose, are nearby. The proximity of these wonderful stretches of water, combined with local beauty spots such as the Tegg's Nose summit, makes the area very attractive to walkers and fishermen.

TRENTABANK RESERVOIR

Trentabank is a key nature reserve boasting a heronry, with more than 20 nesting pairs. The reservoir is one of four collecting water from the hills at the head of the River Bollin. The main area of water reaches a depth of 6oft (18m) but the south, east and north-east banks have shallow margins. In addition to the herons there are colonies of crossbills, goldcrests and, in the spring, pied flycatchers.

RIDGEGATE RESERVOIR

Rusting pipes beside the Ridgegate Reservoir (right). The view is due north, looking into the depths of the Macclesfield Forest. Here forest paths are numerous enabling the visitor to enjoy dappled sunlight on hot days after the sweltering heat of the lakeside paths.